HOW WE ARE CALLED

A Meditation Anthology

MARY BENARD AND KIRSTIE ANDERSON

EDITORS

SKINNER HOUSE BOOKS

BOSTON

Printed in the United States.

Cover design by Kimberly Glyder.
Text design by Suzanne Morgan.

print ISBN: 978-1-55896-446-4
eBook ISBN: 978-1-55896-632-1

6 5 4 3 2
15 14 13 12

Library of Congress Cataloging-in-Publication Data

How we are called : a meditation anthology / edited by Mary Benard and Kirstie Anderson.
     p.cm.
  ISBN 1-55896-446-0 (alk. paper)
    1. Meditations. I. Benard, Mary. II. Anderson, Kirstie.

BL624.2.H69 2002
291.4'32—dc21   2002030865

TABLE OF CONTENTS

Unitarian Universalists draw from many wells of inspiration, from the wisdom of women and men across the ages and cultures and faith traditions, and on our religious journeys we are always open to new paths that might lead to sources of deeper truth. *How We Are Called* embodies this diversity by providing new meditations from a wide range of writers. We are called in many ways, by many voices.

As a Unitarian Universalist I have long had a deep appreciation of the written word's importance to our religious movement. And the longer I serve as the editor of *UU World* magazine, the deeper my appreciation grows, particularly my appreciation for the religious power of writing, which helps illuminate the mysteries beyond human knowing, realities we cannot touch or hear or see or taste.

Through meditation on the cornucopia of illuminating writing this volume presents, deep truths can bubble closer to the surface. As I turned the pages, I was drawn to a particularly homely metaphor—the wooden backscratcher, a stick with a curved end and little carved fingers that allows us to scratch itches we can't reach with our own. In these pages the secret religious meaning of this object is revealed. In fact, if you look at a wooden backscratcher just right, it might even reveal a Unitarian Universalist understanding of what some traditions call original sin.

It is likely that you will find a different favorite, and this is good. It is the Unitarian Universalist way, each of us drawing truths from the sources nearest our own hearts. This meditation manual calls us to services in a small metaphorical congregation, and as we reflect on the readings of the members already present we are invited to join with them, to learn in our own ways from them as we do from our interactions in the congregations we attend on Sundays.

The writers of this volume are clergy and lay people; they are poets and writers of prose. May they provide you paths to many fresh springs of inspiration.

TOM STITES

THIS IS HOW WE ARE CALLED

In the hours before the birds
stream airborne
with chiming voice,
a silent breath rests in the pines,
and upholds the surface of the lake
as if it were a fragile bubble
in the very hand of God.

And I think,
this is how we are called.

To cup our hands and hold
this peace,
even when the sirens begin,
even when sorrow cries out, old and gnarled,
even when words grow fangs and rend.

Cupped hands
gently open,
supporting peace
like the golden hollow of a singing bowl,
like the towering rim of mountains
cradling
this slumbering and mist-draped valley.

KIMBERLY BEYER-NELSON

MOONLIGHT IN THE FROST

Frozen leaves crunched beneath my boots and plumes of condensed breath fogged my glasses as I crept along a deer path under the full moon of a pre-dawn November morning. Warm summer breezes filled with singing cardinals and buzzing hummingbirds seemed an eternity away. To hear or see owls was the reason I was in the woods before daylight on a morning of heavy frost and subfreezing temperatures.

While I was fortunate enough to see a Great Horned Owl that morning not twenty feet away, it wasn't the large, yellow-eyed predator that profoundly stirred my soul but an inconspicuous sight on the forest floor. Looking down to pick my way through the woods, I noticed faint lights among the leaves. Since the nearest artificial light was some distance away, I stopped and knelt to examine this strange luminescence. When I reached down to touch one of the points of light, it disappeared. Withdrawing my hand made the light reappear. Slowly, I realized that each individual crystal of frost on the leaves reflected a tiny, perfect full moon. I'll never know whether it was the position of the moon in the sky or the angle of moonlight shining through the bare trees—but the narrow deer path I followed into the woods was illuminated faintly by moonlight reflected on frost crystals. A Milky Way galaxy in miniature stretched before me here in the woods of Iredell County, North Carolina, on an icy November morning, pointing the way to . . . just pointing the way.

It seemed almost sacrilegious to step on such a perfect example of duality: heaven and earth, black and white, yin and yang, light and darkness. Both ancient and modern Tao teachers, attempting to explain to students their place in the cosmos, silently point one hand at the sky and the other at the ground. This simple, profound act signifies that humanity's place is between the heavens and the earth. The traditional Taoist maxim "Heaven, Earth, Humanity" places the importance of heaven and earth before that of humanity, reminding us that we are only a part of everything under the skies and on the earth.

I followed that path into the woods that morning. May we all be fortunate enough to have a path shown us by the universe, and may we all have the courage to follow it. Enlightenment need not arrive all at once, straddling a bolt of lightning, or even after a lifetime of meditation and study. It might come in small packages, as moonlight reflected in the frost of a cold November morning.

DANNY SWICEGOOD

TO FILL THE VOID

I do not care if your true god controls
the whole sweet universe or just your own
small piece of it. Your god may fit black holes
and worms in some grand scheme and rule alone
or with a multitude of jealous gods
or spirits of wild animals and trees.
This god may want you sacrificed, or awed
by sacred myths, or praying on your knees.
That god may let you meditate or smoke
cigars and twirl around. You may prefer
a god or goddess, think it's all a joke—
there is no god, just science, cold and pure.
Just tell me you belong, your faith's enough
to let you sleep at night, despite sure death.

MARY ZOLL

THE SONG OF THE SOUL OF THE EARTH

A true story
Sings
The Song of the Soul of the Earth
And we feel it
Deep in our bodies,
And deep in our souls,

Because
The Song of the Soul of the Earth
Is our song too.

If you ride your breath
And quiet your mind,
You will hear
The heartbeat of the Earth.
You will feel
The ebb and flow of the tides
In the push and pull
Of the blood beneath your skin.

The air you breathe out
Joins the breezes
That circle the Earth,
And when you breathe in,
The air in China
Stirs ever so slightly.

Where do we begin?
Where do we end?
When we take in
The things around us,
What we leave behind
Changes everything.

A mindful moment
Sings
The Song of the Soul of the Earth

And we feel it
Deep in our bodies,
And deep in our souls,
Because
The Song of the Soul of the Earth
Is our song too.

SUSAN PODEBRADSKY

CLEANING THE KITCHEN

The Japanese master Nan-in once hosted a re-
nowned professor who wanted to discuss the basic
concepts of Zen. The professor freely shared his
ideas while Nan-in prepared tea.

Then Nan-in began serving. He poured his
visitor's cup full and kept pouring, so that tea
overflowed onto the table. Still, he kept pouring.

The professor, stunned, burst out, "But it is full.
No more will go in!"

"You are full," Nan-in said, "full of your own
opinions and speculations. How can I show you Zen
unless you first empty your cup?"

Bernie Glassman says, in *Instructions to the Cook*,
"We always begin by cleaning. Even if the kitchen
looks clean, we still have to clean it again each time
we want to start a new meal." We are told to clean

the kitchen before cooking, while cooking, and after cooking.

These are in fact regulations for Zen monasteries that date back a thousand years, and they are meant literally. Cleanliness is prized in the Zen monastery. It is part of the aesthetic of simplicity, part of being attentive to what is before us.

But it is also a metaphor for cleaning the mind. Before we do anything, we meditate or otherwise center ourselves, often first thing in the morning. We meditate while we cook the meal of our life; that is, we maintain awareness. At the end of the day we reflect upon our actions, making sure we have cleaned up any messes we have made, making every effort to maintain simplicity and harmony in all our relationships. We do what we can to stay open and in touch.

Actually cleaning the real and tangible kitchen is also a form of meditation, the kind of task that is sometimes easier to concentrate on than sitting meditation. Nothing to it. Simply mop the floor. Nothing else. No planning the next meal just now, no evaluating the last meal, no wishing for ingredients we do not have or rehearsing grievances or worrying, no opinions or speculations. Just empty the teacup, wash the floor.

No hurry, no need to get anywhere. There is nothing to attain, just this moment of watching the mop, enjoying the warmth and security of home, the

reflection of your face in the soapsuds. Just washing.
All joy is contained in this moment. If you are not
perfectly happy now, when will you be?

JEANNE DESY

BREAD SACRAMENT

Punching into
lifting out of
rolling   pulling
wrestling with my angel
in the warm sanctuary
of my witch's kitchen,
my charged hands
shape the living dough.

My soul loafs
as the pungent yeast
buds and branches,
instar after instar
until the pans are full.

A complex message
rises slowly up out of
the old blue oven,
a message of winter wheat
in the golden heat of early summer,

of new bread to be held high,
consecrated,

eaten with fervor
and shavings of butter.

LOIS ANN CARRIER

BE LIKE WATER

run deep run clear

fill any space to its own dimensions
respond to the moon, to gravity

change colors with the light

hold your temperature longer than the surrounding
air
take the coast by storm

go under ground

bend light
be the one thing people need, even when they're
fasting

eat boulders, quietly

be a universal solvent

KENDRA FORD

THE GIFT

The house finch sings
his new living space
into being under the same sun
that powers my song.
Sun and song pour down
after the hard white blaze
of oblique winter light.

He has chosen the blue spruce
I once called mine
because I planted it. His mate
weaves and waits deep within
while he sings his seven syllables
seven times or more
from the spirea bush.

When I have learned them,
he flicks his tail and adds a syllable
or two, or sings in run-on lines,
or trills before and after the caesura.

And I grow rich and easy
as less and less belongs to me.

LOIS ANN CARRIER

REST BY ME

"I, the Rock, I, the River, I, the Tree, I am Yours . . ."
—MAYA ANGELOU

Come sit by my side, under my shade,
settle for a while in the summer garden
that I have made for you. You who
have labored hard with hands, hearts and
minds, come and I will give you rest.

Rise up slowly and come. Put down your
daily, weekly and monthly planners. Turn
off your cell phones and beepers. Disconnect
your e-mail and cradle your PalmPilots. Take off
your watch and see only my outstretched arms,
look gently upon my green filigree
fingers as they touch blue sky.

This is my time, I am the goddess of the green,
the god of unearned grace. Come to me
and I will give you rest.

No ticket is needed to enter my sanctuary.
No creed need be recited or promise pronounced.
A prayerful open heart will gain you admission
to my river banks of green, my cathedral columns
topped with green, my meadows radiant with green.

Do not bring lists of entertaining things to do.
I will provide all the amusements you need.
In my green house there are dancing water-striders
on still waters, racing river rapids, the motion pictures
of crashing waves and meandering streams.

Come and I will give you rest.

STEVE SHICK

JOURNEYING

On long journeys, I find the tools and maps I need
are tucked away beneath the surface of things, there,
in the crannies between rocks and in secret pockets
of land and my own heart; there, where mist curls
around the base of mountains and fog covers valleys
and in the sweet places where rivers run, a tumult of
 water
and sound; there, where I find green moss grows
and the heron lifts its wings and sacred trees stand.

Where I have found levers, a compass, a sextant
to guide me and scale the night sky, the horizon
 beckons
away from home to no place I have known,
yet the earth and its markings are familiar; the
 red clay

gashes forth from brown earth and the dim light
glows.
I can measure my steps from here to there
in months and years and countless joys and pains,
the sorrows of parting from lovers and the songs of
love aroused,
requited, and failed, a landscape that echoes the
altitude of grief,
the latitude of learning, the longitude of love.

I have found my footsteps from years before, where I
placed
my feet in climbing rocks or stood barefoot in sand,
the place where I held you, and where you touched
me,
there in my heart, there on my face, there in my
mind.
I could not bear the weight of such memories on my
own
nor know how to transcribe them, but for the voices
of Chesapeake, Huron, and Genesee.
Somehow the rush of rivers circumscribes,
and waterfalls and oceans surround, the place where
I confront me.

In my knapsack of suede and blue, where I collect
such souvenirs as shells, stones, and feathers,
these unsettled tools of wisdom atop clothing and
notebooks and pens,

I carry something beyond the physical evidence of
    travel,
harboring the echo of voice and image of heart
that taught me to grieve and allowed me to see
how hearts could merge and divide,
where a journey of many steps stopped with one
    movement,
a shift from love to acceptance, with no resolution.
I remain a witness to our joining, finding my path
Open with learning once grief is lost from the map
    of love.

ELIZABETH FAUE

INSTRUCTIONS

Where you live now, you will rouse from each night's
darkness when the delivery arrives. Then, as the
eastern sky pinks up like a newborn, the birds will
fill the air with song. In a world of sound and light
and precious breath, you will open the package.
Your task is to use its contents.

No day's box is like another, nor is any person's.
Usually, but not always, you will find everything
you need. Often there will be more than you need,
and discovering ways to use it will be a trial and a
delight.

Comparing your box with another's will give you both pleasure and pain. Desire is a condition of your life, and you will often want what you do not have. Sometimes you can trade. You will be tempted to steal. You will protect yourself from theft.

You will try to save one day's leftovers for another day. Sometimes you will succeed. Other times you will see what you did not use swept into a great heap of waste, gone forever, and you will feel regret at the loss.

Your fellows—and you, yourself—will judge what you do with the contents of your box. These judgments will sometimes bring satisfaction, sometimes dismay, and you will wrestle with them continually.

You ask me what to do. I remain silent. In darkness I fill the boxes and in light you open them.

MARCIA LEWTON

BUT MOSTLY LIFE IS LIKE THIS

Sometimes life is like this. A minister friend, Meg, was invited to moderate a forum between two groups that, truth be told, would each rather that the other not exist. One side spoke and shouted. The other side spoke and shouted. Words passed like light—invasive and all encompassing, but little understood. Exhausted, the combatants turned to

Meg: "Have you anything to add?" Meg rose. "If you are in this camp, God loves you. If you are in that camp, God loves you." Then she sat down. Grace abounds.

Sometimes life is like this. I once went to a meeting with my District Executive in Delaware. Assuming I knew her position, I joked with her. "Oh yes, I'm a Unitarian Universalist Christian, but my Christology is appropriately low." "What is wrong with a high Christology?" she demanded. Two weeks later, I learned that she left our place for a Catholic place. Assuming I knew her position, I forgot to hear her voice. Assuming I knew her position, I forgot to invite her into conversation. Presumption abounds.

But mostly life is like this. On a Thursday after-noon, I said to one I value and trust, "Should we go to the water for the day? Spend some time on the bay?" "Yes, I think so." We drove. She sang the songs of her childhood. We watched a sunset. We heard a dog bark. The boats slowly made their way under the bridge. A Navy pilot navigated his craft. The woman at the Back Creek Inn gave us directions to a café, where we were served wine and laughter. Life abounds.

ROGER BUTTS

Who is God on a bad day? I'll tell you who God is: He's the guy washing a piece of fruit over the sink, only the fruit has ants on it. He's using a spray hose to blast the ants off the fruit and down the drain. We're the ants.

Sometimes he goes to the extra trouble to blast-blast-blast an ant who had almost gotten away.

Who is God on an ordinary day? God is the pesky reminder that turns into the possibility of insight. It's like cleaning your kitchen before the in-laws come over. As you kneel down to clean off the front of the oven, you notice some old dried pudding stuck to the kitchen cabinet, down near the floor.

You get down on your hands and knees to clean the dried pudding from the cabinet, and from that angle you look up and see all the dust on the window, the crumbs in the corner, the chipped formica, all the little bits of crud attached to things you move through daily, all the stuff you've been living with. It's all been there this whole time—for weeks, months maybe.

You see some of this for the first time. You wonder what visitors to your house might see. And you shudder with disgust or fear or a new resolve to clean things up. But some things are too cheaply made to ever look good. And in another month the dirt will just be back again. Thanks for the fresh insight, God.

Who is God on a pretty good day? You look up from what you are doing and notice someone—your spouse, someone you know, perhaps a stranger. And God is the thought: *You know, I gotta be nice to somebody; it might as well be you.*

Who is God on a great day? God is the excuse to say thank you. Dear God, Thank you for this life. Thank you for my spouse. Thank you for my family and friends. Thank you for my congregation, my calling, my colleagues. Thank you for this day—this amazing, never-to-be-repeated day. Thank you for another day of living. Thank you for all the blessings in my life, known or unknown to me. Thank you. Thank you. Thank you. Amen.

DANIEL Ó CONNELL

APRIL FOOLS

Spirit of Life and Love,
We gather on this day dedicated to fools and whimsy.

We do not know who created this day,
But surely it was a wise soul,
Hardly a fool.

For there are indeed days that come to us all,
When we are one with the Trickster,

Delighting in the world of surprise and laughter,
And it lightens our spirits.

Then there are days
When it feels that the joke must surely be on us,
When we wonder if there are other fools like us in
  the world:
Clowns whose smiles are not so different from their
  frowns.

But the good news is that there are—
We are all fools of a kind,
And not just once a year.
We have foolish hearts that dare to love,
Foolish minds that dare to explore,
Foolish spirits that dare to dream—
Look around!
We do not live by reason alone.
We need something more.

So let us pause for a moment,
To be grateful for the fools
Who live in each of us.

Let us not be afraid to let them out,
To laugh and fall and stand again,
For we can never know what wisdom
We might yet learn.

LISA FRIEDMAN

THE VIRTUES OF CROOKEDNESS

In our society, a person leading an "upright" life follows "the straight and narrow," while a depraved person is "twisted" or "warped." Synonyms of "straight" include honest, moral, and virtuous. "Crooked" is equated with corrupt, deceitful, and treacherous.

To straighten my feet, the pediatrician prescribed corrective shoes. I hated them. In summer I ran barefoot, which the doctor deemed therapeutic—an opinion I joyfully accepted. By August, my calloused soles could withstand even the tacky mid-afternoon asphalt. But the dreaded shoes returned with the shortening days. Today, my feet still head off at obtuse angles from each another, as if my big toes were mutually repellent. I know that my parents were well intentioned, but I wonder whether the outcome would have been different had my body followed its own, uncorrected path.

Often I was admonished to "stand up straight" by parents, teachers, and coaches. Each time, I hid my shame, grittily pulled back my shoulders, and promised myself that this time I'd remember. Grown-ups called me "round-shouldered" to embarrass or cajole me into spinal rectitude. Today, my posture remains poor, and I still wince when I catch my stooped reflection in a mirror. Quickly, I straighten my back and repeat the childhood promise. My wife must notice, but in our twenty-five years together she has never told me to "stand up straight." Her silence has been one of the greatest acts of acceptance and love in my life.

The efforts to align my anatomy included my mouth. In sixth grade, I faced the orthodontist. After pulling four molars to "make room" for the impending reformation, he added braces and headgear (a contraption that was mercifully imposed only at night). These were followed by years of wearing a retainer, a piece of plastic molded to the shape of my palate, which was physically inconspicuous but garbled my speech.

Even my eyes had the wrong curvature. I was the only kid in kindergarten to wear glasses. A wonderfully kind teacher managed to convince the other children that I was lucky to have such a grown-up device. By elementary school, the astigmatism had accelerated so rapidly that the ophthalmologist prescribed hard contact lenses to apply pressure to my eyes and prevent further deformation. So even my eyes had braces.

Genetics being a fickle transmitter of form, my son inherited few of my misshapen parts, while my daughter has my teeth, eyes, and oddly shaped pinky finger. This last feature comes from my mother's side of the family. The tendon running beneath my little finger is too short, which prevents it from being fully extended. I like to think that this curvature predisposes my hand to taking hold of another's. When I look at my daughter's hand, I see my mother's, passed through me. My mother is an artist; I am a scientist—there is no straight line to be drawn from my mother to me, no linear extrapolation that can predict what my daughter will become. Twisting to see backward and stooping to peer forward, it seems that bodies and lives are curved.

Straightness is overrated.

JEFFREY A. LOCKWOOD

THE THRILL OF BEING UPRIGHT

I remember the day my son, Scott, stood for the first time. He carefully pulled himself up against the recliner and turned to me with the most beautiful smile of accomplishment a proud father could ever hope to see. His limited world had suddenly expanded to three and a half feet high—counting his reach. And he seemed more thrilled than I. He immediately sensed the new power that standing had given him. His hands were free to manipulate and carry things—a big improvement over crawling around with toys in his mouth, cat style. Maybe he was just excited about becoming more like his parents. In his own way, he had joined the land of adults, and the new range of options and choices he'd created was clearly compelling and satisfying. . . .

. . . Until evening. By nightfall he had become so intoxicated by the power and thrill of standing (and shuffling around the house, balancing against walls and chairs) that he could not permit himself to lie down and sleep—even when he was completely exhausted. Far into the night the battle of competing drives continued mercilessly: He wanted desperately to go to sleep, but the thrill of being upright would not let him lie down.

Every two minutes or so this cycle would repeat: Exhausted, he would lie down, but almost instantly, he would miss standing! So he would begin to whimper and cry and pull himself up again. The later it got, the more tired he became and the worse he felt—as the cycle continued toward midnight. Still, he would not release himself from his dilemma. Every soothing tactic I tried—songs, back rubs, bottle, rocking—failed. Every time I put him back in the crib the anguish returned, until eventually I realized that I could not be his savior. He was going to have to fight this battle alone.

As I sat in the rocker next to his bed, his tender, innocent tears synchronized with my own, and I realized that he was feeling, for the first time, the

bittersweet dilemma of humanity. He was caught
between the desire to soar and his physical limits.
The day of his biggest triumph had also brought his
biggest grief. He had felt the full force of what it is
to be human: that the thrill of being upright will not
let us easily lie down.

The next morning, I awoke to coos and screams
of joy. Scott was standing again.

PAUL KISMITH

NOVEMBER

I feed myself.
I listen to the rain
falling bright and furious.
Rain remembers its falling for a moment, rippling,
then forgets itself in the sheeting, sliding, silence.

It's four-forty.
The sky reflects gray in the windows across the alley.
I know my life is not
and will not be
profound
but I adore it anyway—
    book strewn and poorly fed
    over-thought and occasionally betrayed;
I adore it.

It doesn't matter that the difference
between myself and the rain
is a matter of a little salt and some organization.
I love my skin and all it contains until the rain falls
    through it.

And I'll love it even then, if I may.

KENDRA FORD

DANCING IN THE WIND

Except for a few stubborn holdouts
the tree outside my window
is bare of leaves.
The wind,
this October morning,
worries those few remaining leaves,
pulling them this way,
twisting them that way,
tugging at them
until, one by one,
exhausted by the ceaseless effort to hang on,
they go dancing with the wind.
As they waltz past my window,
the stubbornness has left them
and they are finally free.
What is it about living things

that we expend so much energy resisting the
   inevitable,
hanging on to that which is already gone,
hoping to sustain a season
into times that are unseasonable,
clinging to old habits
despite the pain and discomfort?
Why are we so afraid to dance in the wind?

DAVID BUMBAUGH

THE VASE

My friend tells this story. He had been sharing an
apartment with a roommate for several years. The
roommate had many exquisite belongings: oriental
rugs, Chinese imported porcelain, Sheraton furniture, and Steuben glass. Most of these objects had
been acquired when the roommate had shared his
life with a lover, who had since left him. Somehow
that made these things precious to the roommate,
and my friend knew it. In a way, the apartment had
become a memorial to this failed relationship.

One night, my friend stopped at a florist on the
way home from work and bought some large lilies.
When he got home, he looked around for something
to put them in, and he spied the perfect vase, a tall,

elegant vase that had been one of the last gifts from the former lover. My friend arranged the flowers, put them on the mantle, and went about making dinner. All was well—at least until the warmth of the house started to open more and more of the blossoms, shifting their weight. My friend was in the kitchen when he heard the vase hit the stone hearth.

This was a disaster. My friend knew his roommate would be devastated. The vase was irreplaceable. He swept up the shards of glass, trying to decide whether to play dumb ("Vase? What vase?") or plead for mercy. He chose the latter.

The roommate got home. The story was told. There were no fireworks, no tears, no anguish. Just a quiet, calm acceptance of what had happened—a kind of forgiveness, a kind of letting go. The next day, the roommate called an antiques dealer and sold most of the furniture he had preserved from the broken past. He rolled up the carpets and took them to an auction. He gave the rest of the Steuben glass to friends who had admired it. And he thanked my friend for choosing that particular vase to hold the lilies.

It wouldn't have worked out the same way if the roommate had smashed the vase in anger. The ending would have been different if my friend had avoided revealing a painful truth. But several things serendipitously came together: the choice of the flowers, the selection of the vase, the placement on the mantel, the warmth of the furnace, the readiness of the roommate to reconsider the life choices he had made.

The disaster was really a blessing. From an unwanted event came an invitation to freedom. It doesn't always work that way, but this story is a reminder that it's possible. It's possible for disappointment to open doors we had been afraid to enter. It's possible that the past won't let us live in the present. It's possible that everything makes its own sense, even when that sense is not immediately clear to us. When life's next catastrophe sends you reeling, sit down and take a few deep breaths, and see what happens if you peel away the layers of meaning to see what is pulsing at the core. Maybe you too will find reason to give thanks in an unlikely occasion.

DAVID S. BLANCHARD

SALVATION

It was fall. Bee season was nearly over. Surely his best days had been spent. He was sluggish, the way bees get in the fall when the temperature drops and the pollen has been harvested. Yet he patiently and methodically explored my window pane, searching for a way out. Through the hazy consciousness of pain medication (I had just had surgery), I was only peripherally aware of his quest for the outdoors. When the sun set, his buzzing stopped and I forgot all about him until the next day.

On the second day, he resumed his effort to extricate himself from my house. All morning he continued to search my window in an attempt to fly free into the bright sunshine and blue sky, which always seems especially bright and blue on a fifty-degree autumn day. More alert today, I began to marvel at his persistence even as I contemplated such mundane questions as "Where did he spend the night?"

Finally, I realized that I could help him escape. I hobbled over to the window on my newly bandaged and sore feet, carrying a plastic cup and a used envelope. Careful not to crush him, and almost twice catching a wing, I managed to encircle him with the cup. Slowly I worked the envelope over the cup's opening. Only then did I realize that should he break loose and try to sting me, I wouldn't be able to run.

Slowly I hobbled toward the front door. Once on the porch, before I could savor the moment of his release, he escaped into the vast outdoors, that place he had been trying to get to for at least two days.

No doubt the circumstances that freed him were far beyond his comprehension. This is what salvation is like for people, too.

PETER HOUSE

I DO NOT HAVE A PERSONAL RELATIONSHIP WITH GOD

I do not have a Personal Relationship with God.
   I've lost his phone number;
   he never answers his mail.

We did not, as young men,
   hang out on Wednesday nights,
   cigarettes dripping from our lips,
   at pool halls.

He is not there like an old neighbor
   to fix my broken lawn mower
   and hand me a soda
   on a blazing hot day.

When I rip my shin on a jutting shelf
   and cry out his name,
   he does not rush to me
   with Band-Aids and peroxide.

He does not, at times of vexation,
   when my world lies shattered,
   my relationships ruptured,
   my children insolent,
   my finances hopeless,
   come with soothing counsel to my side.

He does not take my requests
    like a long-distance dedication
    on America's Top Forty,
    or deliver within five business days
    or my money back
    on my catalogue order—
        my business is not important to him.

I do not have a Personal Relationship with God.

But in quiet moments—
    in the familiar whistle
    of a red-winged blackbird on a cattail,
    or in spider webs glinting with dew
    in the grass of a clear sunrise,
    or the passing attention of an old cat—
        He/She/It/Whatever does not
        speak
            or do
                or answer
        but admits me to fleeting union
        with the Greater.

PATRICK MURFIN

THE CHURCH WHERE EVERYTHING GOES WRONG

Six weeks into the church year, I have realized that I am the minister of a church where things usually go wrong. This morning the copy machine jams repeatedly. The bulletin describing the order of worship has been copied with the second page first and also upside down. No one has remembered to turn on the lights in the sanctuary before the service, so it is dark because it is raining outside. The microphone is buzzing and every so often lets out a painful, high-pitched squeal that makes people wince. We have just started the service when someone runs up with a bunch of flowers for the altar, just as someone else runs in with one of the silk arrangements we keep for the mornings when no one brings real flowers. There is laughter as the two flower bearers meet at the altar. They decide on the real flowers, and things settle down for a while until one of the babies starts crying, which sets off another baby crying. I try to speak over the wailing as their fathers hustle them down the aisle and try to distract them in the back. Usually, I love watching the tall, gentle fathers who bounce their babies in backpacks at the rear of the sanctuary, but today I am annoyed because I want it to be quiet and holy and lovely and things are definitely not shaping up that way.

The woman who is helping with worship gets up and, instead of giving the announcements, introduces the candle-lighting time, which comes later. People call out, "Not yet!" More laughter. The organist starts playing the wrong hymn and a couple of choir members yell over the din for him to stop; a few minutes later, during the period for prayerful silence, he accidentally falls onto the keyboard, causing the organ to emit horrible, gassy noises. Shrieks and snorts of laughter. All pretense of Sunday morning decorum is lost and something inside me, some furious, bossy desire to have "my worship service" go according to my plan, finally slides free and I laugh with them.

This will be the first of many times that I laugh at Sunday morning details gone awry. It is also the first of many times that I imagine that God is watching, looking up or down or over or out at us from wherever God sits on Sunday mornings, slightly amazed and maybe at a loss for words because we, God's people, are so funny and wonderful and odd all at the same time. In moments like these I imagine God as a sturdy old woman with her hands on her hips, or perhaps as a rabbi pulling on his long, white beard. I imagine a God shaking his or her head and saying, "What in the world are they doing over there? This is what they call church? What were they thinking?"

But I also imagine a God who is touched and maybe a little honored by our efforts, however halting, to worship and give praise. I imagine a God who is moved by our attempts to care for one another and to name the things we know as holy. There is a warmth in this congregation that is new to me, a simple friendliness that shines through the fumblings and failures, a love that makes the ragged edges smooth. I have always wanted to believe, really believe, that our mistakes aren't the most important parts of us. I have always wanted to believe that kindness and compassion matter more than anything. I sense that I can learn this here.

ELEA KEMLER

BACK-SCRATCHER

The fall from grace,
    the great disruption of primordial order,
        the original sin, had nothing to do
            with eating apples or talking with snakes.
The instrument of our fall was a wooden back-
scratcher,
    that piece of wood, bent at the end
        so one can reach the unreachable spot—
            there, between the shoulder blades,

down just a little bit lower,
now up a little bit,
there where the most persistent itch
always takes up residence.

Before the back-scratcher,
before that simple, infernal device,
we, like all our primate kin, depended on others to
    do for us
what we could not do for ourselves:
"You scratch my back, I'll scratch yours."
Before the back-scratcher,
before that simple, infernal tool,
we needed each other to scratch the unreachable
    itch.
The wooden back-scratcher dissolved the bonds of
    reciprocity,
    unloosed the ties of community,
and tempted us to believe in our own godlike self-
    sufficiency.

And God walked in the cool of the garden,
and saw a primate standing alone.

"What have you done," God asked, "that you stand
    alone?"
"I have found a back-scratcher," said the beast,
"and now I need no one."
"Poor beast," said God, "now you must leave this
    garden:

"In Eden, no one stands alone; each depends on
the others."

And thus began our wandering, our pacing up and
    down the earth,
scratching our own itches, pretending self-sufficiency,
trying to ignore the persistent sense of loss,
the vague yearning for a primordial order,
a world where you scratched my back and I
    scratched yours.

A wooden back-scratcher is poor compensation
for the gentle touch of a living hand.

DAVID BUMBAUGH

FAIRY GODMOTHER

I've appointed myself a fairy godmother. I carry
stars in my wallet, not the lick-it-yourself kind from
when I was a kid, but those newfangled self-stick
kind that come in sheets of gold, silver, red, and
blue. When I saw a man at the ATM machine take
the previous customer's card out of the machine
and walk over and hand it to her through the car
window, I waited until he'd finished his transaction.
You know, people can get kind of squirrelly at those
ATMs if you approach too closely. When he turned

around, I whipped out my stars, selected a gold one, told him he'd earned a gold star for doing such a nice thing, and stuck it on his shirt. He was silent, and I thought perhaps he was shy or didn't understand my gesture. Then he got into his car and I heard him say, "That's the nicest thing that's ever happened to me."

Another time in the grocery store, a woman a few aisles over in the checkout line must have picked up more groceries than she had planned and was balancing them precariously in her full arms. The man in front of her noticed and moved the groceries in his shopping cart around to make room for hers. I whipped out my stars, ran over between the candy racks to him and told him he'd earned a star and could pick out whichever color he wanted. He smiled a toothy smile, selected a red one, and stuck it on his hand. The woman behind him smiled, the cashier smiled, all the people waiting in the other lines smiled, and I smiled too.

I have never had anyone refuse a star from me. I have seen big, scary-looking people melt, pride blossoming in their eyes, remembering the days in first grade when they got assignments back with a gold star at the top. I have thought about encouraging recipients of my stars to pass the star on to someone else when they witness an act of kindness. Someday a star might find its way back to me here in

Charlotte, North Carolina, or I might hear of someone wearing one in California. There might be a whole band of fairy godmothers and godfathers, and people would realize that the way we treat each other really does make a difference.

KRISSA PALMER

ANGELS IN SMALL PLACES

Some people think that angels always come heralded—glowing brightly, trumpets sounding, with an angelic choir in the background.

Me, I think angels mostly come in small places—like the friendly clerk at the fast food place who makes you laugh on that day when you thought it wasn't possible, the homeless man in the shelter who teaches you about the portability of dignity, the friend who refuses to stop caring as you become a teary mess, the acquaintance who drops just the right word at the right time and makes a bridge of hope.

Sometimes, your angels don't even need to be alive anymore to give aid.

I hardly think my great-grandmother qualifies for typical angel or saint material. Married three times, she outlived two husbands and kicked a third out when she lost patience with his alcoholism. When she died at 85, she left me an engagement ring from another fellow who wanted to marry her. She'd declined, saying she'd had enough of marriage.

But she never tired of loving. She knew how to build hope. When my much abused father was kicked out by his parents at 16, she took him into her home. There, he finished high school, then went off to fight in World War II. Shortly after my parents married, she asked them to move in with her to help her out. She gave him enough love so that he loved also.

I was fortunate enough to live with my great-grandmother for the first four years of my life. One of my favorite pictures of her was taken outside, with my brother sitting on one side of her and me on the other. I'm holding onto her skirts and looking out, seeing what there is to explore out there. Under her tutelage, I climbed to the top of the kitchen cabinets, frightening my mother out of her wits, but avoiding any harm to myself. I followed the dog into the woods—and safely back out. Where my mother feared, my great-grandmother had tired of fear and decided she was through with it at her advanced age.

For various reasons, I was very troubled and confused as a young adult in college. One night, I dreamed it was the year 1890 and I was twenty-five, the same age as my great-grandmother. She let me rest inside her mind as she danced and laughed and

rejoiced in life. The next day, I was calm, as if the
storm had passed, leaving me weaker but still
standing. I'm still not quite sure if it was really a
dream or if she came back one last time to help.

If I'm very lucky and work at it, maybe I can leave
a little bit of that kind of legacy for someone else.

KAY FRAZIER

THE CREATION OF WOMAN

I'm standing in your kitchen, Grandmother.
You and my mother are busy with late-morning
    housewifery.
The breakfast dishes are nestled in their cupboards.
The August sun has heated the corrugated tin cellar
    door;
Already it's too hot for sliding down.

So I've been drawn inside to the aromatic chaos of
    your kitchen.
The evaporative cooler droning away in the front
    room provides the only relief
from the dry West Texas wind.
You are so very large,
oh, mother of mother, forbidding to one so small.
Yet you reach to hug me and I am lost in your
    enveloping flesh,

Your damp cotton dress sticking to us both.

Your large form rises from your throne at the end of
the table.
Oh, Great Mother,
I watch in awe as you slap down the risen dough,
punch and knead and form it,
Thou, Creatrix of the Universe,
Your huge arms and strong hands creating new
shapes,
recognizable forms in miniature of our staff of life.

Sitting again, sighing under your own immense
weight,
You catch sight of me and pull me close once more
in a sweaty hug.
Then, holding my broad little face in your damp
hands,
Your countenance brightens in self-recognition
and you call to my mother over your shoulder,
never dropping your gaze from my eyes, every bit as
green as yours,
"Oh, Margaret, look.
We have made woman in our own image, after our
likeness.
And it is very good!"

I am blessed.

EVA CESKAVA

FROM SONG TO ECHO

Before I came I was in the birdsong
announcing dawn,
in globes of dew
on needles of the spruce
dropping onto fallow fields.

I could hear gulls
spread sound over the sea,
colored blue by dawn light,
and feel swelling water
bounce off the ocean floor.

There in shafts of light
the bones of my ancestors
began to drum an echo,
and to that beat
stone pounded stone upon the shore.

Out of the rock came life,
animals ground seeds;
I inhaled life
in the first breath
that blew through a reed.

My flesh moved
with other hands drawing
rhythm from a skin drum;

knowing hunger in the reach
of an empty bowl.

I wore my beads
and danced on earth's soft face,
gave life, helped children to their feet,
learned from smooth stones
to question my uneven edges.

For a time it is all mine,
until my bones form
instruments for the coming dancers
whose song, whose indecipherable words,
my spirit will come to understand.

JACQUELINE BEAUREGARD

A LITTLE PIECE OF OUR SOULS

Everywhere we go we take our souls with us.
And every time we meet someone we wrap a little
    piece of our souls around them
and pass it through them.
All our lives, we weave our souls
around and through everyone we meet,
tying a complex, tangled web to the earth.
This is who we are to the world around us.

Each of us has a thousand, a million tendrils of
    other souls wrapped
around us and through us.
And this is who we are to ourselves.
Sometimes we need to grasp these tendrils for all
    we're worth
just to keep ourselves here.
Sometimes the tendrils snap
and we can't weave anymore.
But the thousand, the million threads we have
    already woven remain,
tangled messily about the earth.
This is still who we are, and we aren't diminished,
but it does leave a hole.
You have wrapped your soul around me and
    through me a thousand, a million different times.
If I gather all these threads in my hands and hold
    tight,
and if you hold onto all the threads that have ever
    pierced your soul, wrapping them around you like
    a protective cloak, anchoring you to the ground,
maybe the threads won't snap, and you can keep
    weaving a little longer.
If it snaps anyway,
I will take all the threads you have left me
and wrap them around a spool
that I will carry with me always.
But try not to let your tendrils snap.

I'd like to feel you weaving your soul around me
and through me
for a little while longer.

STEVEN F. SMITH

BROKEN SHELL

I remember climbing to see
A robin's egg in a nest
So perfect and beautiful and blue.
Young friends had shown it to me
And warned me to beware:
Only look but do not touch.
I was enticed; it looked like a jewel.
Surely one touch could do no harm?
But the shell fractured and the yolk and white
    leaked out.
Embarrassed, I hid the shell and told no one.

I am sorry for the children
Who returned to view the special egg and found
    nothing.
I am sorry for the mother bird
Whose offspring was never seen.
I am sorry for the life of the bird
Who never even got to become whole.

And it seems to me that most of our sins
Are not out of malice or meanness,
But simply not heeding a warning
And handling something fragile in a clumsy way.

KITTY SCHOOLEY

WHEN I HEARD OF YOUR LOSS I CALLED

Your voice was like shattered crystal
on terrazzo
and I was barefoot
and walked across bleeding
reaching for you with my voice.

And we talked
of cabbages and kings
of why man's blood is boiling hot
and whether broken dreams have wings
and of the lives of galaxies
and turning tears to ink.

I could not speak then of healing
but I thought—
deeper than words I thought—
      Be well.

And slowly
your voice gathered itself together

as if invisible hands
touched rim to bowl to stem
and bid them hold.

PAT KING

BACKPACK

IN MEMORIUM
ELIZABETH IRENE TARBOX
1944-1999

All of the necessities we need for our coming years
of work and laughter
are pared down by your cancer;
all the plans put aside
in the re-sorting to fit
everything into this small space.
Condensed to now,
the future evaporates
out of our cups of ginger tea,
leaving words to keep the dark
from spilling between us.
This backpack full of dreams,
dreams I fasted in order to feed, shifts, throwing
    me off balance.
Now, as I write you a message

in the sand, I hear gulls
laboring the day to dawn
and I am stunned that so much
of the universe survives you
and the sea is its own particular blue.

JACQUELINE BEAUREGARD

STANDING IN THE DARK

Remember, Father, when I was a very little girl
and afraid of the dark,
not because of bears and crocodiles
but because the sky was so wide,
and I called you from the living room,
golden with lamps and voices,
to save me from the hovering questions
that circled the ceiling above my bed:
    But how can the sky go on forever?
    And how many stars are there?
    And if the sky's shaped like a doughnut,
    who's holding the doughnut?
    And if we go to heaven when we die,
    how long will we live up there?
    And what does forever mean?

And you, after a long silence,
    stroking my hair: I don't know.

None of us knows.
But your voice softened the dark
and I never knew when you left the room.

In the years that followed,
after I left home
and you aged and weakened alone,
were you afraid of the dark?
I left the room afraid to ask
before you closed your eyes.

What does it matter, now that you
are past the fear of fear?
It matters now for me:
must I stand in the dark alone?
No. Your grave's no tiny plot
but the green earth and the sea
and the whole wide sky.
They are still and always there
with answers—

most often: I don't know.
But memory ties time together
and again the darkness softens
as if you had never left the room.

PAT KING

At a ministers' retreat someone read a passage from a book about why ministers make people feel uncomfortable. It is because we dress in earth-colored clothes, and when we shake hands with people, we hold their hands a second too long and gaze into their faces and say earnestly, "How *are* you?" All the ministers in the room howled with laughter at the accuracy of this picture.

But the passage went on to say that the real reason people find ministers weird and don't really want us to come to their parties, even if they invite us, is because we are too comfortable with death. Like funeral directors, we don't respect our society's fear of anything related to serious illness and dying. We go striding into hospitals and sick rooms as if the smells of cancer and antiseptic don't make us want to gag, as if it's no big deal to sit down by the bed and hold the dry, skeletal hands of someone who is dying, to watch people gasp out their last breath, to murmur words of comfort to shell-shocked relatives.

One December I buried a baby for the first time, a three-month-old who died of sudden infant death syndrome. The coffin was white and so tiny I couldn't believe anything could be inside. It looked like the kind of Styrofoam cooler you bring to the beach. The parents had come from the Midwest to bury their baby next to his grandparents. At home the day before the funeral, I read the service I had written over and over until I could do it without crying.

On Saturday, the day of the funeral service, there was a snowstorm and the ground was so frozen and snow-covered that we decided to postpone the burial until Monday. Monday morning was sunny and still. The path through the cemetery to the grave was carved out of snow banks packed down so hard that people sat on them like benches while waiting for the family to gather. A square hole had been dug in the ground, the fresh, brown earth vivid against the white snow. Using ropes, the funeral directors slowly lowered the little casket into the hole. I was afraid they would drop it with a thud, but they were careful and the casket gently found the bottom of the hole.

The baby's father was from a Jewish family and he had asked that we say the Kaddish, the mourner's prayer. I did so haltingly, badly, reading the Hebrew from a card the funeral director had given me. Others in the small group recited the prayer from memory, eyes closed, rocking gently back and forth on their feet. Then each person took a turn shoveling dirt onto the casket with a small shovel. The baby's mother went last. She did not take the shovel the funeral director held out to her, but fell to her knees by the grave, sobbing, her head bent almost to the ground, her hands covering her face. Her husband leaned down over her. Her adolescent daughter crouched behind her, resting her head against her mother's back. Nobody moved. It was completely quiet except for the sound of crying. The two funeral directors and I stood across from the family, on the other side of the hole in the ground, like three dark-coated sentries guarding the grief in front of us. It was cold. We stood there for what felt like a long time. Finally, one of the funeral directors, who had a sweet, boyish face and straight straw-colored hair, said gently, "It is time to go now." Slowly, the family rose and turned away from the grave.

I called the sweet-faced funeral director later in the week. I felt as if the family's grief had changed the pull of gravity around me, making the air heavier, like I have to push through it just to move. I was blunt; I asked him how he could stand the sadness day after day. I don't remember what he answered, only that he was kind. I didn't ask him what I really wanted to know—how to make the air around me lighter. I didn't tell him that what I really wanted was to go to a loud bar and get drunk and smoke cigarettes and laugh. I wanted food and loud music and bodies holding each other close. I wanted to forget all about small white coffins and raw holes in the ground and mothers on their knees crying. I was embarrassed by my intense desires. It would be a long time before I began to understand that for me, desire was the pull back to life and I needed to follow it. It would be a long time before I learned to respect and listen to my body's craving for pleasure in the face of loss, before I understood that it is all right, even good, to remind myself, after I have stood close to death once again, that I am still alive.

ELEA KEMLER

MEMORIAL FOR A FRIEND

My leaves are falling,
A few at a time,
More at a time, many,
Into a pile of gold that was once my dress.

My leaves pour down.
I am naked.
Every knob shows, every scar,
The place where thugs broke off my best branch.

I stand here plain.
Black bark.
Roots. Roots.
My leaves are piled around me.

My roots have gone deep in the clay,
Moving things around, displacing stone.

Above me is nothing. I am nothing.
The thugs have gone home with my branch.

There are no birds.
No song.
No caress of beak and claw.
Nor is there blight, scab, pest, disease, or rot.

Nothing to hide from,
Nothing to defend against,
Nothing to reach for.
I sink down in the snow.

How strange that it turns out this way.
No thoughts about reaching.
No sorry sentiment over the shaking of my
    golden skirt.
I need not dwell on fruit.

I let myself sink. My feet are deep.
The earth pulls me down into this deep dwelling.
This is it. This is now. This is today.
Tomorrow is something else.

MARCIA LEWTON

O God of Justice and Righteousness, Goddess of Compassion and Peace, form an alliance to sustain and strengthen us in this time of our anguish and travail. Help us to understand that the horrible images we see over and over again will fade, in time, into tranquil landscapes and portraits of courage.

O God of the Eternal Tides and Goddess of the Evening Stars, bring to us assurance of the confident and reliable rhythms of life and the serenity of safe nights.

In this terrible time of testing wills and tempting vengeance, give us the words to soothe and comfort one another, to promise the children that we will always be near, to pledge to the grieving the healing balm of our sympathy and hope, and to offer those who are anxious and afraid a calm and abiding trust in love's consecrating power.

O God of Strength, Goddess of Enfolding Care, combine your skills to steer us through the turbulent storm. Crack our hardened hearts so that we may see again the light of divinity in each human soul. Help us to reject blind retribution and despair. Focus our vision on a world cradled in peace and help us to dedicate our lives to the work of the preservation and proclamation of freedom and justice for all.

O God of Life, O Goddess of Light, we ask for
your benediction upon the innocent lives lost, the
families torn asunder, and upon our country in
need of the resuscitation of its heart and the recu-
peration of its soul. Give the sustenance of peace to
a world whose eyes have seen too much of terror
and violence and not enough of reason and loving-
kindness.

Grant us wisdom to sheathe the sword of anger,
and courage to proclaim liberty to the captives of
fear. Grant us wisdom. Grant us courage—for the
facing of this hour.

Amen.

BRUCE M. CLARY

REVELATION OF A GENESIS

So it happened that bombs fell
until there was no creed left
to detonate more;
then the bones of every culture
dropped into a sea as uncontainable as hate.
This era of silk ties and tents,
begging hands, military medals,
cars that cost years of a poor man's labor, This time
    ran out of time—

bone fragments falling through water,
arrowing down toward a dark without shadow.

But there was a lightness in the ash,
spirit lying in petaled layers,
a presence on the water's skin,
a spirit lifted by fog to a kingfisher nest
near the crown of a spruce,
its boughs cupped upward.

Spirit that came to lie
within the concealment
of a needled cocoon
a nest whose lining held filaments
of blossoms and beasts,
seeds of earth, feathers
of the king of fishers,
that in mysterious fog spilled
into air and spread life.

JACQUELINE BEAUREGARD

A SOLSTICE REFLECTION

"In a dark time the eye begins to see."
—THEODORE ROETHKE

Solstice celebrations capture the moment when the darkness gives way to the light. For thousands of years, people have tried to hold onto that moment of joy and certainty.

Five thousand years ago at Newgrange, in Ireland, people built a circular structure that let a shaft of light travel deep into a central chamber at the dawning of the winter solstice. There, the light pierced the darkness and illuminated intricate symbols, including eye-shaped carvings. We can imagine how the anxiety caused by the approaching darkness was relieved when the light was seen making its journey down the shaft. Then, observers could predict their future with confidence.

In time, after the winter, the growing and harvest seasons would follow.

Constructing shafts for the light to penetrate deeply into the central chamber of our hearts is an effort that must take place in a time of waiting and uncertainty, in a time before "the eye begins to see." It is a time when adjustments need to be made. Christians call it *Advent*, a time to prepare for the arrival of the Son, the light of the world.

So much of what we do in life depends on how we respond to this waiting moment.

Such a time can be met with confidence and anticipation or anxiety and despair; confidence that the light will be seen again, or anxiety that it may never return. We are in such a moment today. Violence, whether we call it war or terrorism, fills our minds. Compassionless public policies gnaw at our hearts as the season of compassion approaches.

What can we do in this waiting moment?

Practice imagining the dawning shaft of light as it makes its way into your own heart. To direct this light requires us to, as Dag Hammarskjöld suggests, "vanish as an end and remain purely as a means." No small task. But if you doubt its effectiveness, think of those who have made a difference in your life and what they have selflessly given you. Or think of the man whose life we celebrate at Christmas. Jesus, it is clear, vanished as an "end" and lived only as a "means."

Join with others. No solitary individual assembled the great circular stones at Newgrange. People gathered together to build a chamber where the light could be reflected in others' eyes. Waiting is not the same as being passive. Living in this dark time requires active waiting.

The only question is: Will we, in this waiting time, build a chamber where the light can be reflected widely enough so that others can see its beauty?

STEVE SHICK

MY PSALM

God of life and love and mystery.
God of one thousand names.

Too much am I Ishmael, crying in the desert.
Where is your face, if you have so many names?
Too much am I Sarah, casting off bad decisions—
banishing
Inconvenience out to the desert to die.
Where is the blessing, if yours is the kingdom at
    hand?
Too much am I Abraham, indecisive, passive in the
face of conflict.
Where is the covenant, if the covenant is for love's
sake alone?

Too much am I in exile, too much in Babylon,
Too much weeping in this foreign land,
And I, far from home, can't sing my holy songs.

So where is the prophet, the teacher, if finally comes
    the poet singing:
"Comfort, O, comfort my people"?

We wait and we wait.

Shake me up in my complacency;
I feel like going on.
Shake me up in my delirium;

I will not be moved.
Quicken in me this sense of love;
I too have a dream.

ROGER BUTTS

ONE WISH

If you had but one wish,
What would it be?

Take your time thinking about it.
So much is at stake—
an end to all suffering,
a stop to all violence,
a solution to poverty and all of its ills.

Would you wish for love?
For forgiveness or for healing?

Would you wish the world joy?
Or the wisdom to change?

Would you wish to understand everything?
Or to know less than you do?

Take your time thinking about it.
So much is at stake.
For a wish is a thought,
And a thought is an idea.

An idea leads to commitment,
And a commitment cries out for action.

A wish can be a dangerous thing,
Something daring.

And it need not be witnessed by the stars
To come true.

Let us be glad that we are not given just one wish in
   our lives,
But many.

Let us be grateful not for wishful thinking,
But for the discipline of the thoughtful wishing
That can lead to change.

What would your wish be?

LISA FRIEDMAN

THE LONG WALK

The best story I ever heard about gift-giving has
nothing to do with Christmas, and everything to do
with Christmas. It's about an African boy who
wanted to give a gift to his teacher, who was going
home to England. The child had no money and his
options were few. The day before the teacher was to
leave, the child brought her a huge seashell. The

teacher asked the boy where he could have found such a shell. He told her there was only one spot where such extraordinary shells could be found, and when he named the place, a certain bay many miles away, the teacher was speechless.

"Why . . . why, it's gorgeous . . . wonderful, but you shouldn't have gone all that way to get a gift for me." His eyes brightening, the boy answered, "Long walk part of gift."

"Long walk part of gift." Most of the meaningful gifts we give to each other require some version of that "long walk." The long walk we sign on for with children, who need our patience, our wisdom, our honesty, and our trust more than we might first have imagined when their lives began. The long walk we share with our spouses, which takes us through uncharted, unexpected territories of sickness and health, richer and poorer, better and worse. The long walk we take with our friends when they are grieving the loss of someone they love, when they are ill, when they are discouraged. The long walk of feeling a sense of unity with those whom prosperity has left behind. The long walk of reconciliation with all that separates us from a deep sense of life's great purpose and meaning. "Long walk part of gift."

When Christmas has been tidied up and packed away for another year, the gifts acknowledged, many already forgotten, the New Year stretches in front of us. What will get us through those months, with all that they may hold, will not be the things in the boxes. We must look to the hands of those who bought and wrapped and carried those gifts. With their gifts, they are telling us something too wonderful, perhaps too embarrassing, for words. They are telling us that, for us, they will take the long walk.

So when you open the box and find the chainsaw, the long underwear, the fruitcake, the pot holder, or the seashell from a distant ocean, remember that it's not just "the thought" that counts. Remember too, "long walk part of gift."

DAVID S. BLANCHARD

VIETNAMESE CHRISTMAS

My most meaningful Christmas—up to my preemie's first in 1985—was in the 1960s when I lived with my missionary parents in Vietnam. I was still in elementary school then.

We were one of the last American families to be evacuated.

That year was meant to be the best Christmas ever for me and my siblings. The double barrels of food, clothes, and toys from our stateside families had actually arrived on time for once. We had good things to eat, new clothes that fit and toys fresh off the shelves. One aunt had even sent us a string of lights and a small generator to power them. We kids were in happiness overtime . . . until Christmas Eve, when someone blew up our house.

We escaped with our lives and pajamas. The American government folks drove us straight to the airport to get us out of the country. Right before we boarded our plane to the Philippines, an elderly Vietnamese woman came up and handed my mother a bag. My mom, expecting another bomb, immediately told us to run and scatter. She tried to shove the bag back at the woman.

But this wise old woman whispered to her, "My grandson blew your house up. I could not stop him or turn him in. In this bag is a Christmas gift and clothes for each member of your family."

That gesture fixed it some then and fixed it all later as I have grown older.

My son's best friends now are Vietnamese-Americans. It is within the realm of possibility that their families and ours might be connected by that night. Either way, we are connected spiritually.

Someday I mean to return to Vietnam. When I do, I'll carry clothes and gifts for as many elderly women as I can. I owe that grandmother this much.

RUS COOPER-DOWDA

HOLY KITCHEN

Don't ask me why I am alone today,
This day when almost everyone else
Makes an enormous effort to be with family.
It is my choice, for many reasons,
And all is well.

Here I stand, in my own familiar, newish kitchen,
Preparing, without any real need to do so,
The ceremonial dishes of my tribe.

My sense of the presence of those departed is sharper
In my solitude.
I know they come whenever I use this bowl,
Prepare this recipe,
Wait just this long and then do that.
Today there is no chatter to distract me,
No live guests eager for the result
Of this process.

I am more attentive to the spirit.
Lingering in the comfort of the ritual,
My thoughts and gestures start a conversation
With the hovering shades.
They speak in silence—and I listen—
And when they are silent again,
Their lingering blessings remain,
Settling gently in this place,

Leaving it forever changed,
Ever so gently charged with holiness.

MARY WELLEMEYER

23 LATKES

I am sitting at my desk here in my bedroom thinking
about Hanukkah.

I have all the potatoes, sweet onion, flour, sour
cream, and applesauce I need for latkes. I have the cut-
up inside-out brown paper grocery bags to drain them
on. I have the foil to keep them warm in the oven. I
also have the sweet pastry my family loves. A few gifts
must still be wrapped in the traditional blue and white.

But it would take a lot more than all this to top a
Hanukkah of a few years back, when my husband
and I were invited to what we thought was a potluck
dinner. The host family consisted of three adults,
three kids, and a tangle of playful kittens underfoot.

We brought a medium-sized jar of applesauce, a
small container of sour cream, butter, and a single
loaf of homemade bread. And twenty-three latkes. I
know that we only brought twenty-three latkes
because I counted them as I packed them up .

When we got there, it turned out that our latkes,
bread, and trimmings were the *only* food. Then the

family invited the upstairs tenants. Then the tenants and their kids invited some friends of theirs who had just stopped by. At one point my spouse and I counted six or eight kids and about as many adults. (Since the kids kept moving all the time, our count was imprecise.)

I and my spouse took the tiniest portions of everything and then watched as everyone dug in. Everybody ate at least two latkes. The kids ate mountains of applesauce. The adults slathered sour cream everywhere, even on the bread. Yet at the end of our visit, there was still leftover sour cream, applesauce, and latkes. The idea that Jesus fed huge crowds twice with simple, small lunches of fish and bread suddenly looked more feasible to me.

Our friends and their neighbors ate until they had had their fill. We were filled with the miracle that took place. And we all parted satisfied.

And that's how we were reminded of wonders we cannot understand but for which we should be grateful.

RUS COOPER-DOWDA

THE REALLY INTERESTING THINGS
HAPPENED 12 BILLION YEARS AGO

This is nothing at all,
nothing more than the moon's reflection sprawled
across a rippled pond, a physical
manifestation of something distant. Meanwhile, the
    universe
spreads and thins. One day, it will likely reverse
itself, collapse, coerced
by gravity, but for now, I wait, wonder
about antimatter, the forces that tear stars asunder,
the astounding number
of photons trapped in black holes, particles freezing
in deep space. Everything cools—
no time to question the wisdom of breathing.

MARY ZOLL

Unitarians and Universalists have been publishing prayer collections and meditation manuals for more than 170 years. In 1841 the Unitarians broke with their tradition of addressing only theological topics and published *Short Prayers for the Morning and Evening of Every Day in the Week, with Occasional Prayers and Thanksgivings*. Over the years, the Unitarians published many more volumes of prayers, including Theodore Parker's selections. In 1938 *Gaining a Radiant Faith* by Henry H. Saunderson launched the tradition of an annual Lenten manual.

Several Universalist collections appeared in the early nineteenth century. A comprehensive Book of Prayers was published in 1839, featuring both public and private devotions. Like the Unitarians, the Universalists published Lenten manuals, and in the 1950s they complemented this series with Advent manuals.

Since 1961, the year the Unitarians and Universalists consolidated, the Lenten manual has evolved into a meditation manual.

For a complete list of meditation manuals, please visit www.uua.org/skinner/meditation